O s &

Tatiana

Dear Oscar and Tatiana,

I miss you both a lot. After our phone call I really felt like packing my suitcase and going to join you at Grandpa and Grandma's house.

I know that you would have rather stayed at home this vacation, but being alone is just too dangerous. It's safer for you to be at Grandpa's house. You will have fun.

One more thing – it is too expensive to call on the phone. I am sending you some writing paper, envelopes, and stamps. I am also sending some new crayons and drawing paper for Tati. Write soon!

Love,
Mom

Dear Mom,

Thanks for the package! What a great idea! I'm taking good care of Tati like I always do.

Yesterday, we helped Grandma work in the vegetable garden. We dug up onions, potatoes, and carrots. We washed everything well and then Grandpa showed us how to make his famous vegetable soup. Tati would not even taste it because she had seen a worm in the dirt. Grandma told us that earthworms make the soil healthy. When she told Tati to take a little taste, Tati started to cry. Tati made you a picture.

Love,
Oscar

P.S. Do you remember Grandpa's famous vegetable soup? Did you eat it?

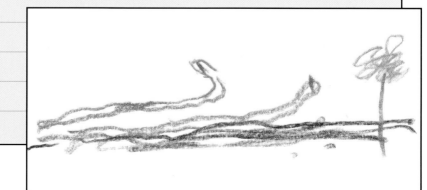

Dear Oscar and Tatiana,

Thanks for the card and Tati's picture. Yes, I do remember Grandpa's soup. He made it every time anyone was sick. If I get the flu, you can make it for me. Tati, I understand how you feel about the worms. I used to work in that same vegetable garden when I was a kid. Those worms are very wiggly!

At work we had a party to celebrate the holidays. We had a secret gift exchange. I received the same scarf that I had given away as a present last year! It was funny. The house seems very quiet when you're not around. Write back soon. I miss you!

Love,
Mom

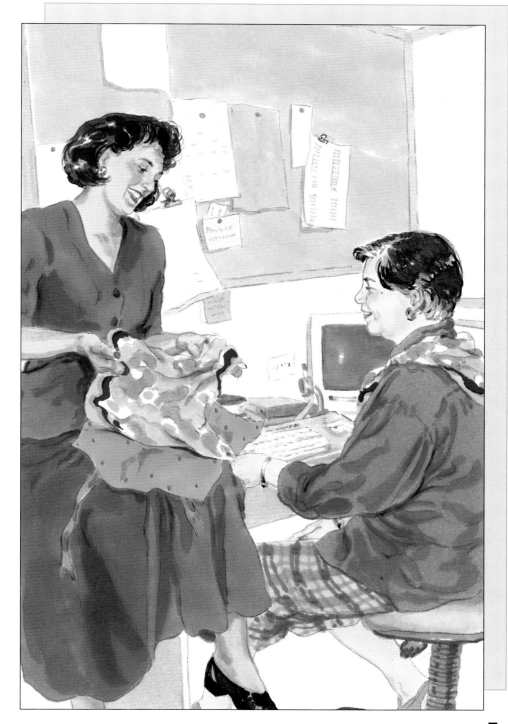

Dear Mom,

   We are all fine today. Yesterday Tati got in trouble when she tripped over a paint can and spilled white paint all over the green grass. Grandpa had asked us to stay away while he touched up the fence, but Tati kept running all over the place and didn't see the can. It was a big mess, Grandpa was not happy. Tati is crying all the time. Here is her drawing.

                I miss you, Mom!
                         Oscar

Dear Oscar and Tatiana,

Thank you for all the letters. It makes me happy to find a letter in the mailbox when I come back home from work. Oscar, try not to worry about Tati's crying. She just gets that way when things are new or different. Do you remember her first week in kindergarten? She cried if she had to wear a sweater and she cried when she had to fold a paper. She'll grow out of it. You used to cry, too, you know. We all cry at times.

I am already packed, even though there's still lots to do before I can join everyone.

Much love,
Mom

P.S. If Grandpa is not finished painting, please stay away!

Dear Mom,

Grandpa gave us a huge box of old photographs. While he watched the game on television, he gave us a job to do. We had to separate the photographs into groups. He wanted baby pictures in one pile, pictures of grown-ups in another pile, pictures of old people in the last pile. When the game on TV was over, Grandpa checked our work. He said we did a good job. Then he put all the photographs back in the box and we went out for ice cream. We miss you. Tati sends a big kiss and this picture.

Love,
Oscar

P.S. Why did we have to sort all those photographs? I can't figure it out. I think I'll ask Grandpa.

Dear Oscar and Tatiana,

Well, you fell for one of Grandpa's oldest tricks! Sorting is Grandpa's way to get you out of his hair. When I was a kid, he used to have me separate all kinds of stuff, just so I wouldn't bother him. While he and Grandma would play cards, I had to sort another deck by color and suit and then put them in order from start to finish.

Only a little longer to wait! I miss you both. Tati, thanks for the picture.

Love,
Mom

Dear Mom,

Today we walked to the park. Grandma was fine, but Grandpa had to rest three times. He said he couldn't walk as much as last year and looked a little sad. Tati told him not to worry because she would buy him some skates and a cane for Christmas. We started laughing so much we all had to rest. That's when Tati started to cry. Tati never cries at home. I think she really misses you. Here is Tati's drawing.

I can't wait to see you,
Oscar

P.S. Tati told me that Grandpa is at least one million years old. How old is he, really?

Dear Oscar and Tatiana,

I would really love to see Grandpa in roller skates! I laughed just thinking about it. Thank you for the letter and Tati's picture. I am so glad that you have a chance to spend some time with your grandparents. I'm really not sure how old Grandpa is. He would never tell me. But Grandpa loves to play guessing games. You might try to trick him by playing a guessing game about his age.

Much love,
Mom

P.S. Don't ask Grandma about Grandpa's age. She won't tell you either.

Dear Mom,

Tati fell and scraped her knee. Grandma cleaned it up and put a bandage on the scrape, but Tati would not stop crying. I gave her a hug and sang her the song you always sing when we're hurt. She finally stopped crying. Grandpa was watching. His eyes got very shiny. He came over and told me he was proud of the way I took care of Tati. I felt important, Mom. Grandpa told me that he used to sing that same song to you when you were little. Here is Tati's drawing.

I love you and miss you,
Oscar

P.S. Have you ever seen Grandpa cry?

Dear Oscar and Tatiana,

Oscar, I'm proud of you, too. You do take good care of yourself and your sister. You don't need to write to me anymore! Guess why! I got all my work finished and my boss has agreed to let me leave two days early to join you! I can't wait. I just know I'm going to cry when I see you, so tell Grandpa to bring plenty of tissues to the station.

I'll be there in a couple of days. If you get tired of waiting, ask Grandpa to do his paper trick for you. See you soon.

Much love,
Mom